HALTOM CITY PUBLIC LIBRARY
3 1751 00158 4672

D1162317

RACE CAR LEGENDS

The Allisons

Mario Andretti

Crashes & Collisions

Drag Racing

Dale Earnhardt

Formula One Racing

A.J. Foyt

Jeff Gordon

Motorcycles

Richard Petty

The Unsers

Women in Racing

CHELSEA HOUSE PUBLISHERS

Shell

RACE CAR LEGENDS

FORMULA ONE RACING

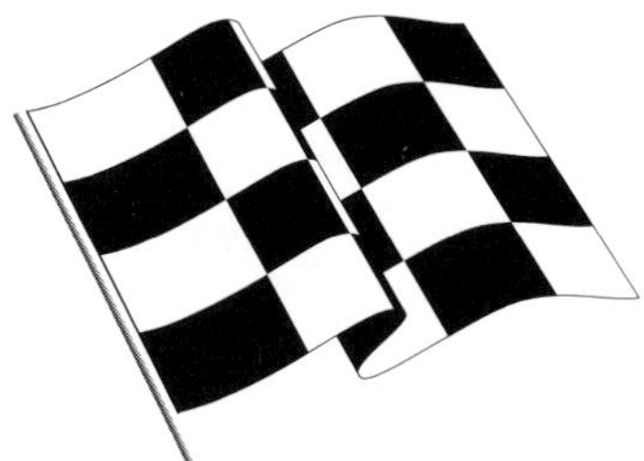

Richard Huff

CHELSEA HOUSE PUBLISHERS
Philadelphia

Produced by Daniel Bial and Associates
New York, New York

Picture research by Alan Gottlieb
Cover design by Takashi Takahashi
Cover photo: Britain's Damon Hill winning the Australian Grand Prix in October 1996. Credit: Popper foto
Frontispiece photo: Michael Schumacher

3 5 7 9 8 6 4 2

Library of Congress Cataloging-in-Publication Data

Huff, Richard M.
Formula One Racing/Richard Huff.
p. cm. —(Race Car Legends)
Includes bibliographical references (p.) and index.
Summary: Tells the story of three stars of Formula One Racing, the fastest sport in the world.
ISBN 0-7910-4431-9 (hc)
1. Automobile racing drivers—Biography—Juvenile literature. 2. Grand Prix Racing—Juvenile literature. [1. Schumacher, Michael, 1969- 2. Senna, Ayrton, 1960-1994. 3. Villeneuve, Jacques. 4. Automobile racing drivers. 5. Automobile racing.]
I. Title. II. Series.
GV1032.A1H84 1997
796.72'0922—dc21
[B]

97-21716
CIP
AC

CONTENTS

THE DRIVE TO WIN

What's the most popular spectator sport in the United States? It's not baseball, football, basketball, or even horse racing. America's favorite sport is automobile racing.

To the outsider, it looks simple. You get in your car, keep the accelerator depressed as you hurtle around the track, expect your crew to keep the car in perfect condition, and try not to go deaf as you weave your machine through traffic toward the checkered flag. But in actuality, it's not at all easy. Just as baseball isn't simply a matter of hitting the ball, so racing is full of subtleties.

What does it take to be a world-class race car driver? The more you know about the lives of the greats, the more it becomes clear that each successful driver is an extraordinary athlete gifted with unusual vision, coordination, and the will to win. The concentration necessary to send a car speeding around a track at 200 miles per hour for hour after hour, when a momentary lapse can cause instant death for him and any unfortunate driver near him, is phenomenal. Any driver worth his salt must be strong, self-confident, resilient, and willing to take risks in order to have an opportunity to win.

In addition, the top drivers have to be good businessmen and know how to put together a winning team. They have to find sponsors to put them in competitive cars. They rely on a pit crew to make sure that their car is always in peak performance condition. And they have to be mentally prepared each race day to take into consideration a host of factors: weather, the other racers, the condition of the track, and how their car is responding on that day. Without everything right, a driver won't stand a chance of winning.

The drivers in the Race Car Legends series grew up around

race cars. The fathers of Richard Petty and Dale Earnhardt were very successful race car drivers themselves. A. J. Foyt's father was a part-time racer and a full-time mechanic; the Allisons and Unsers are an extended family of racers. Only Mario Andretti's father disapproved of his son's racing. Yet Mario and his twin brother Aldo devoted themselves to racing at a young age.

Despite the knowledge and connection a family can provide, few of the legendary racers portrayed in this series met with immediate success. They needed to prove themselves in sprint cars or midget cars before they were allowed to get behind the wheel of a contending stock car or a phenomenally expensive Indy car. They needed to be tested in the tough races on the hardscrabble tracks before they learned enough to handle the race situations at Daytona or the Brickyard. They needed to learn how to get the most out of whatever vehicle they were piloting, including knowing how to fix an engine in the wee hours of the night before a big race.

A driver also has to learn to face adversity, because crashes often take the lives of friends or relatives. Indeed, every driver has been lucky at one point or another to survive a scare or a bad accident. "We've had our tragedies, but what family hasn't?" remarked the mother of Al and Bobby Unser. "I don't blame racing. I love racing as our whole family has."

What each driver has proved is that success in this most grueling sport takes commitment. Walter Payton, the great football running back, and Paul Newman, star of many blockbuster movies, have both taken up racing—and proved they have some talent behind the wheel. Still, it's evident that neither has been able to provide the devotion it takes to be successful at the highest levels.

To be a great driver, racing has to be in your blood.

elf
MINOL
E
SCHUMACHER
Ford
Ford
TECHNOGYM
BELL
DEKRA
TECHNOGYM
Ford

1 DRIVING WITH THE KING

On the morning of June 2, 1996, Spain's King Juan Carlos wanted to take a spin around the Circuit de Catalunya, the Formula One Grand Prix course located in Barcelona. His Royal Highness had his pick of the top Formula One drivers, and for that matter, of some of the best auto racers in the world. But he chose Michael Schumacher, a two-time Formula One champion and perhaps the best overall driver in all of motorsports.

Of course, Schumacher could not take the king in his Ferrari Formula One car. Unlike American stock cars, Formula One cars are designed to seat just one person—the driver. And because the cars are so low to the ground, the speeds they attain, which are similar to those of stock cars, seem faster to the driver.

After the quick spin, Juan Carlos made no statement on how he enjoyed traveling at

Michael Schumacher waves his arm in victory after winning the 1996 Spanish Grand Prix.

180-200 miles per hour. For the king, as it would be for almost all people, traveling at such high speeds was a combination of exhiliration and pure fear. For Schumacher, it was just another day behind the wheel, a preparation for the race later in the day.

It was a cold, rainy day, downright miserable conditions for racing. While other forms of motor-sports only race under perfect weather conditions, Formula One events are held rain or shine. Barcelona marked the seventh stop, or round, of the 16-race season. Schumacher, a nine-time winner in 1995, had yet to win his first race of the year going into the Spanish Grand Prix.

A dominant force during the previous two seasons, Schumacher had been hobbled by a car that was not performing well for most of the season. Historically, the Ferrari team had put phenomenal cars on the track. But this year, Schumacher's bad luck could mostly be attributed to ill-handling equipment that had failed. This year, he had only earned two second-place finishes and one third—well off his championship pace. Now he was a distant third in the battle for the drivers' championship. Williams-Renault driver Damon Hill and his teammate Jacques Villeneuve owned the top two spots.

The Spanish Grand Prix is held on a 2.937-mile circuit that has been in place since 1991 and was a focal point for Barcelona's Summer Olympics in 1992. Drivers are not overly fond of the circuit and often claim that its rough surface makes it difficult to get the car set up for optimum driving conditions.

Nevertheless, Schumacher was at home on the circuit. And with the rain falling, he was in

his element. Schumacher excels in bad racing conditions.

At the start, Villeneuve passed polesitter Hill and shot into the lead. Schumacher, starting in third place, struggled.

"It was a disaster," Schumacher said. "I almost stalled the car. I was going for the clutch and there was nothing there. A lot of people passed me and I couldn't see anything. I was afraid I would go into someone."

Further problems arose. "I did have an electrical problem on the 33rd lap which got worse and worse with the car only firing on eight or nine cylinders," he said. The trouble cleared up and then returned for the last 20 laps, causing

Jacques Villeneuve (left) jumps out to a lead at the Belgian Grand Prix. Michael Schumacher (center) came back to win this exciting race. Damon Hill, Villeneuve teammate, is at right.

him to lose speed on the straights. Schumacher feared the car wouldn't finish the race. He was also cold and uncomfortable. Still, Schumacher is always determined and worked his way through the crowd.

Up ahead was Villeneuve. His teammate Hill spun and fell back to fifth and then spun again, dropping him to eighth. Schumacher drove through the falling rain and the spray thrown off the tires of his competitors to pass second-place driver Jean Alesi on lap nine and then took the lead away from Villeneuve on lap 12.

By lap 17, Schumacher had padded his lead by 17 seconds. By the middle of the race, he was notching laps some four seconds faster than his best competitors. Without the serious trouble he'd faced earlier in the season, Schumacher attacked the raceway, much to the delight of the 53,000 fans who had braved the weather to watch the race.

Crashes and mechanical difficulty shortened many a driver's day. Only 6 of the 20 cars that started the race completed the event. Schumacher held on and led each of the remaining laps, finishing the 65-circuit event in first for his 20th career win. It was the first for Ferrari in over a year and only its second since 1990. Alesi finished second followed by Villeneuve.

"It's amazing. If anyone had said I would have won this race, I would not have put a penny on it," Schumacher said afterward. "However, in the morning warm-up, I felt the car was perfectly prepared."

Leaving Barcelona, Schumacher had moved up in the points standings to tie with Villeneuve for second, although Hill had a comfortable lead over both men. Schumacher was grateful to

Juan Carlos. "I would like to take the King of Spain round the track [at the next race in] Canada after he brought me so much luck in Barcelona," the reigning World Champion said.

YEAR
USAG
CHAMPION
Lpr
USAG
M. Schumacher
Rothmans

DRIVING FOR FUN

Michael Schumacher was born on January 3, 1969, in Hurth-Hermulheim, Germany, to Rolf and Elizabeth. Shortly after his birth, the family moved to Kerpen, a city of 54,000 people outside of Cologne, Germany, near the Belgium border.

Rolf was a bricklayer by trade who also managed the local go-kart race track. Schumacher's mother was a cook who spent weekends working in the track's snack bar. Schumacher's younger brother, Ralf, spent weekends tagging along with the family.

Michael took his first laps at age four in a pedal-powered kart his father had built for him. Before long he'd progressed to gas-powered vehicles and by age six he was the local track champion.

Back then, racing for the Schumacher family was pure fun. Indeed, at such a young age,

Michael Schumacher celebrates his victory at the 1995 Monaco Grand Prix as Prince Rainier of Monaco applauds. To the right is second-place finisher Damon Hill.

Michael had yet to consider racing a career path. He was an average student at the local school, but in his early teens he was a superb soccer player.

When he wasn't in school, Michael could be found at the Kerpen track either racing or helping his family. When he got older, he spent his after-school hours working as an apprentice at a local Volkswagen garage.

In 1980, Rolf and Elizabeth took their sons to Nivelles, Belgium, to watch the World Kart Championships. Michael was 11 at the time and watched in awe as a 16-year-old driver worked his way around the track to finish second. That driver was Ayrton Senna, a native of Brazil who would go on to win three Formula One World Championships. Senna's kart-driving prowess inspired Schumacher, who returned home to Germany and dedicated himself to dominating all his competition.

In 1984 and 1985 Schumacher was the German Junior Champion and was third in the Junior World Championships. A year later, racing in the senior division, he was both the German and European karting champion.

In 1988, Schumacher was offered a chance to drive on the FF1600 circuit. He had no trouble adapting to the Ford-powered cars. He finished his first season fourth in the German FF1600 rankings and second in the European division. A year later he moved to the German Formula Three series, where he was teamed with Heinz-Harald Frentzen and Karl Wendlinger, two drivers who would also eventually make the move to Formula One racing. Wendlinger won the championship that year followed by Frentzen and Schumacher.

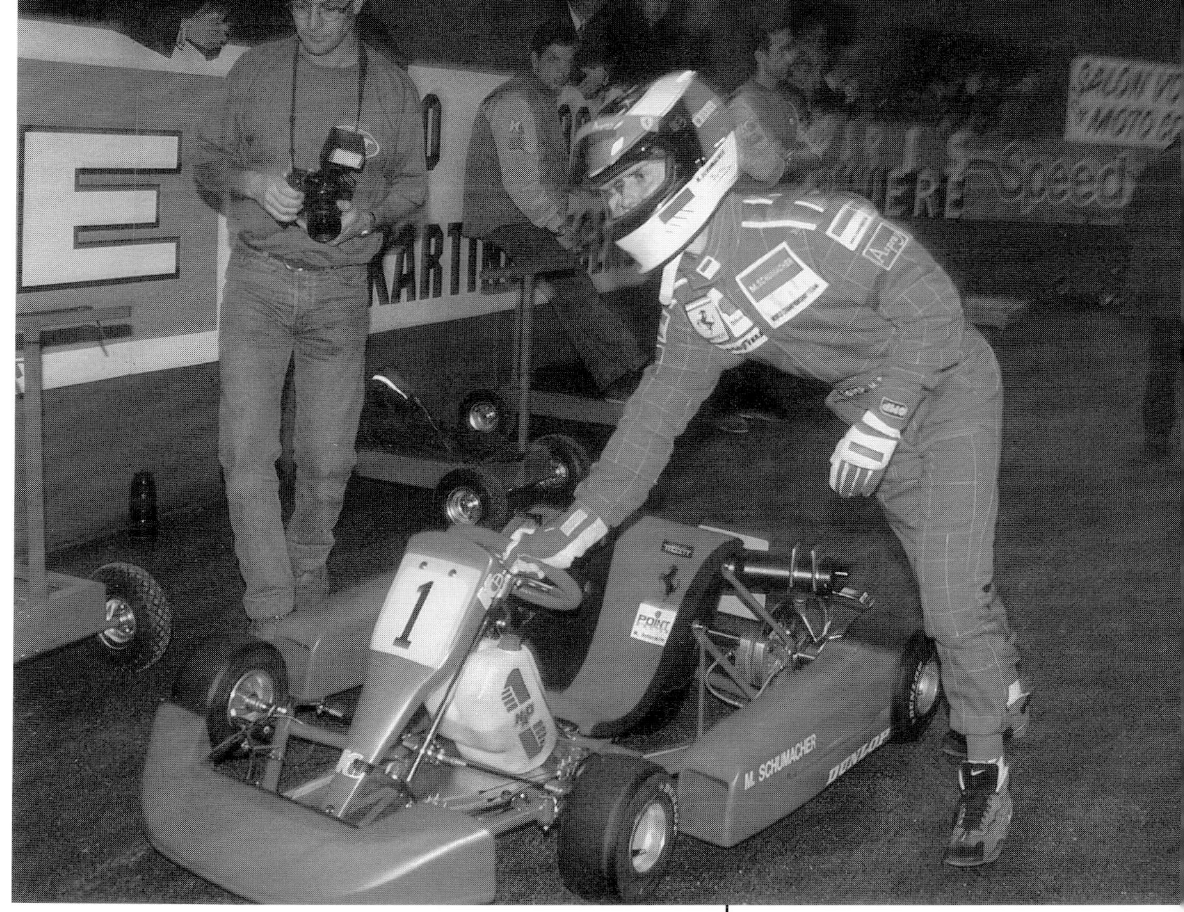

Schumacher's first love as a driver was karts. Even in 1996, he took time off his Formula One schedule to enter a kart race.

Schumacher, Wendlinger, and Frentzen were soon spotted by executives at Mercedes, who signed all three for the automaker's Junior Racing team and started grooming them for the big leagues. As members of the team, all three learned English and how to behave in front of the media.

Schumacher won the German Formula Three title in 1990 and that same year, while driving for Mercedes, won a race in Mexico. Schumacher has said that it wasn't until he was about 20 that he really considered racing to be a career.

Schumacher got his first shot at Formula One in 1991 through a strange turn of events. Team owner Eddie Jordan's regular driver was in jail

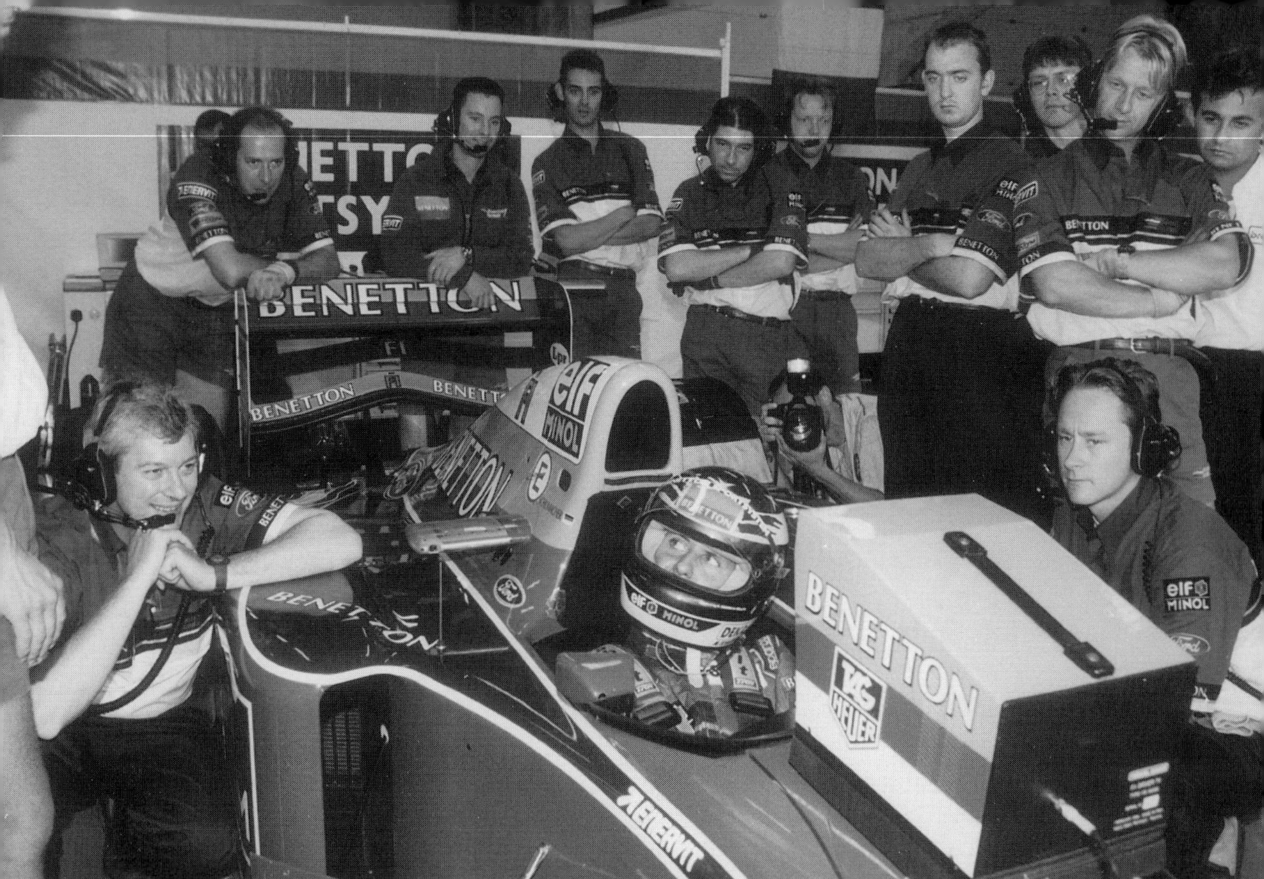

Schumacher sits in his Benetton Ford as his pit crew makes final adjustments before a race.

and unable to race, leaving the car available. Seizing the opportunity, Schumacher's friend, mentor, and manager Willi Weber contacted Jordan, seeking to get Michael a chance at driving. Jordan, unaware of Schumacher's past driving experience, didn't take Weber seriously. Weber persisted and convinced Jordan to let Schumacher take a test run.

"It was a serious risk on our part," Jordan once said. "No one had really heard of him. No one knew how to spell his name."

Schumacher got his first taste of a Formula One car during a test at Silverstone, in Northamptonshire, England. The 3.142-mile long road course is Britain's oldest race circuit in continuous use. Michael did not let the opportunity go to waste. He zipped around the course so fast a team manager is said to have radioed to him numerous times to tell him to slow down.

At 22, Schumacher made his full-fledged Formula One debut in the Belgian Grand Prix at the Spa-Francorchamps, a 4.334-mile-long track, which is the longest on the F1 circuit. Having never been to the track, let alone driven a race car on it, Schumacher set out on a bicycle to learn the layout of the facility.

After the first day of practice he was eighth fastest. He was fifth fastest the following day.

However, the race was a bust as he burned out the clutch only 325 feet from the start.

Schumacher's less-than-spectacular debut didn't turn away potential suitors. Through a nasty business squabble, he ended up driving the next race for Benetton-Ford. He finished fifth in Italy and sixth in Portugal and Spain to accumulate enough points to finish 12th in the overall standings.

In 1992, Nigel Mansell totally dominated the Formula One series by winning nine of the 16 races. Schumacher, with one win and three second place finishes, was third overall, ahead of veterans Senna and Gerhard Berger.

Schumacher's early success and his relatively young age may have played a role in his performance in 1993. Some observers suggested that Michael got overly confident after the 1992 season and made some early driving mistakes in 1993. Nevertheless, he won one race and finished second five times and third once, finishing fourth in the championship.

The 1994 season started with several notable driver changes altering the championship landscape. Alain Prost, a four-time world champion, retired, eliminating one of the toughest competitors on the track. Nigel Mansell, the 1992 champion, was in America driving an Indy car, and Ayrton Senna, a three-time champion, was switching from McLaren to the Williams-Renault team.

For Schumacher, the rapid changes put him squarely in the position of being a real contender for the championship. But five races into the season, the Formula One scene changed even more dramatically when tragedy struck twice.

While qualifying for the San Marino Grand Prix at Imola, Italy, Austrian driver Roland Ratzenberger was killed in a wreck. Several drivers, including Senna, did not return to the track when qualifying resumed.

At the start of the San Marino race, two cars collided, sending two wheels into the stands. Four spectators needed medical attention. As a result of the accident, the first five laps of the race were run under caution. When the green flag came out, Senna jumped into the lead with Schumacher a close second.

Two laps later, Senna's car—traveling at 192 mph—careened off the track and slammed into the wall. He died from injuries suffered in the accident.

The race resumed without the drivers knowing the full extent of Senna's condition. Schumacher won the event, although he called it a "hollow" victory because of the tragedy.

Like most drivers, Schumacher was severely shaken by the rapid and violent deaths of two of his on-track competitors. He was behind Senna at the time of the accident and saw it occur. For a short while, he considered quitting. Indeed, he practiced for the next race at Monaco with the understanding that if he felt differently about driving that he would retire. He didn't and continued.

But Formula One's troubles continued at Monaco, where Karl Wendlinger, Schumacher's pal from his earlier racing ventures, suffered severe head injuries in an accident during practice.

Schumacher won the pole and then led every lap to win his fourth straight race of the season. He went on to win six of the first seven races held.

However, trouble found Schumacher again when the team headed to the British Grand Prix at Silverstone in England. During the formation lap to start the race, Schumacher passed Damon Hill, the polesitter, several times. Doing so was a clear violation of Formula One rules. As a result, race officials decided to give him a five-second penalty. He was black flagged, meaning he had to head to the pits. Schumacher and his team ignored the flag. He finished second, although because he ignored the black flag, he was disqualified. The team was fined $500,000 and banned from two races.

Schumacher's ban was to have gone into effect for the following race, the German Grand Prix at Hockenheim. However, fans protested and threatened to make trouble if their home-town hero wasn't allowed to participate. The team protested the two-race penalty and in effect, postponed Schumacher's ban until after Hockenheim. He rewarded the crowd by finishing second.

He then won the Hungarian Grand Prix in Budapest before sitting out two races. Upon his return, Schumacher won the Belgium Grand Prix. Yet his trouble didn't stop. Schumacher's

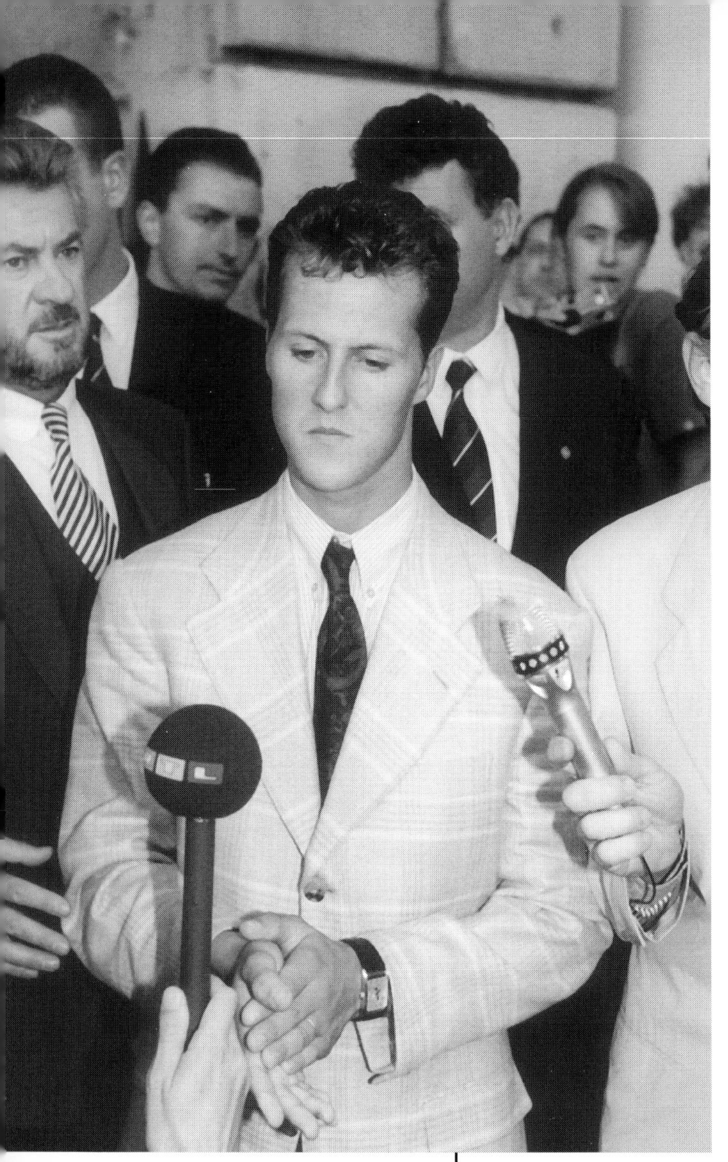

In 1994, Schumacher tried to convince the International Automobile Federation not to suspend him for ignoring a black flag in a previous race. Even though the FIA upheld a two-race ban, Schumacher won the Formula One championship.

team was stripped of its points for two additional races. While Schumacher and his team were fighting with Formula One officials, Damon Hill was able to move back into contention for the championship.

At the European Grand Prix in Jerez, Spain, Schumacher was again victorious. In Japan, Hill was the winner, setting up a last-race battle for the title. The race started with Schumacher ahead by one point. Their hotly-contested battle came to an end on lap 36 when their two cars collided. Both drivers were out of the race and unable to collect points toward the championship. As a result, Schumacher not only won the championship, but at age 25, he was the youngest Formula One champion ever. Of the 12 races he was legally capable of winning, he won seven.

Schumacher's joy at the title was shadowed by the tragic loss of Senna and Ratzenberger and the injury of his friend Wendlinger. "To me it was always clear that I was not going to win the championship and it was Ayrton who was going to win the championship," Schumacher said after winning. "But he hasn't been here for the last races and I'd like to take this championship and give it to him. He is the driver who should have won it. He was the best driver, he had the best car, and those are my feelings about him."

The 1995 season started in Brazil in March, in Senna's birthplace. Schumacher, still riding high over his championship, was unable to shake the controversy that had followed him a season before. He won the race in Brazil, with David Coulthard finishing second. However, both teams were penalized by officials because the fuel they used was not the same as they had told officials they would be using before the race. The fuel wasn't illegal, it just wasn't what officials expected them to use.

Ultimately both teams appealed the ruling and were able to get the driver's points to stand.

Damon Hill won the next race in Argentina, while Schumacher finished third. Hill then took a six-point lead over Schumacher in the points battle when he won the San Marino Grand Prix, the third race of the season. Schumacher rebounded by winning back-to-back races in Spain and Monaco. He won again in Germany and Belgium.

In September, Schumacher announced that he was leaving the Benetton team to drive for Ferrari. According to published reports, he signed for two years worth a combined $50 million. In addition to the driver's salary, Schumacher signed a sponsorship deal with such companies as Canon, Nike, and eight others worth more than $20 million. The deal made him the richest driver in the history of Formula One racing.

"Looking at it now, I would say I'm going to stay about another five years in Formula One," Schumacher said. "But I'm not going to get old in Formula One. Whether it will be five years, or four, or six, I'm not sure yet. As I said in the beginning, I'm going to have fun and as long as I have this I will continue to drive. I might get old in go-karting."

Despite his pending departure from Benetton, Schumacher never let up on his quest for the championship. He notched wins at the European Grand Prix, Pacific, and Japan.

Schumacher secured his second-straight World Championship with two races remaining in the season. He won nine of the 17 races, tying Mansell's record of the most wins for any driver in a single season.

Michael Schumacher entered the 1996 season as the most dominant and feared driver in the world. But back-to-back championships notwithstanding, he knew he would not have the kind of season he was used to. The Ferrari team was clearly in a rebuilding and development year. Before the season started, Schumacher admitted that he probably wouldn't win a race until midway or later in the season.

His claims were justified, although early in the season opener in Australia, Schumacher showed no signs of trouble. He was in third, behind Villeneuve and Hill, when he suffered brake problems and was forced to quit on lap 33.

He finished third at the following race in Brazil, a lap behind the leader. "The weather conditions did not suit our strategy and put us back a bit," Schumacher said. "There is a lot of work in front of us, but we finished and got points. Those were our targets."

Formula One rookie Jacques Villeneuve was able to hold off Schumacher to capture his first

In 1996, Schumacher not only drove for Ferrari, he drove in an all-Ferrari race in Mugello, Italy.

series victory in the European Grand Prix in Nurburgring.

"Jacques drove a fantastic race, without mistakes, and there was no way to pass him," Schumacher said. "He also had the edge on top speed, so there was nowhere I could pass him."

Schumacher followed with a second in the San Marino Grand Prix at Imola. The race was his first in Italy behind the wheel of an Italian-made all-red Ferrari.

Schumacher earned no points in Monaco, but he rebounded with his first win for Ferrari in Spain. His win came in the seventh race, exactly where he had predicted the first win would come. However, the glow of the win didn't last long. He was forced to drop out of the French Grand Prix in Canada early because of mechanical troubles.

"This was really a bad day," he said. "First the fuel pressure was too low, which made it difficult to start the engine. Then the balance of the brakes was inconsistent front to rear, which stopped me from pushing hard. Finally the drive shaft broke which may have caused the clutch problem. . . . I did not expect so many problems all at the same time."

Schumacher's trouble continued for the following two races, until Germany, when he finished fourth.

His problem-plagued season appeared to be continuing at the August running of the Belgium Grand Prix, the 13th race of the season. During practice on Friday before the race, Schumacher lost control of his car and hit a tire barrier, extensively damaging his car. Before the accident, he had set the second fastest time. The crash left the athletic Schumacher with a bruised knee.

He blamed himself for the accident, saying he had entered a turn too fast and lost control.

Villeneuve, who admitted learning the track by playing a video game, won the pole. Villeneuve took the lead and led most of the early part of the race. But Schumacher, showing no signs that his bruised knee was hampering his performance, stayed close.

After a round of pit stops, Schumacher took the lead on lap 21. He turned the lead over to Villeneuve when he pitted on lap 29. But Schumacher took the lead back when Villeneuve brought his car in for service. Villeneuve raced out of the pits just behind Schumacher and dove inside trying to pass on a tricky hairpin corner. Schumacher held his ground and did not give up the lead. He fought off Villeneuve to take his second win of the season.

"It is difficult to find words on how I feel at the moment after all of the problems we have encountered this weekend," Schumacher said. "In the middle of the race I hit one of the curbs and bent my steering. I was frightened in the high speed bends and came close to stopping. . . . The knee I injured in practice proved no problem and I'm just so happy for everybody at Ferrari after all the problems we have encountered."

In doing so, Schumacher notched his 21st win of his short career and proved to the world that he was indeed back on top of his game. Before the season was out he won two more, earning him enough points to finish a distant third behind title winner Damon Hill. He wouldn't win the championship; that title would be left for others. However, he surely would again be a title contender in 1997.

Marlboro
McLAREN INTERNATIONAL
HONDA

AYRTON SENNA

Ayrton Senna da Silva was born in Sao Paulo, Brazil on March 21, 1960. He was the eldest son of Milton da Silva, a former engineer whose business interests included farms and other companies in Brazil, and Neide Senna da Silva. He had an older sister, Viviane, and a younger brother, Leonardo.

When Ayrton was four years old, his father built him a tiny go-kart. Ayrton, then suffering from some minor trouble walking, delighted in going fast.

He started go-kart racing legally at age 13. Most of his competitors, however, would rather he'd never started at all. Senna was a determined racer with an uncanny ability to drive a car on the edge without disaster.

In 1973, in a Junior Class 1 kart at Interlagos (Sao Paulo), Senna participated in his first race and earned his first victory. A year later,

Ayrton Senna gives the thumbs-up sign after winning yet another race.

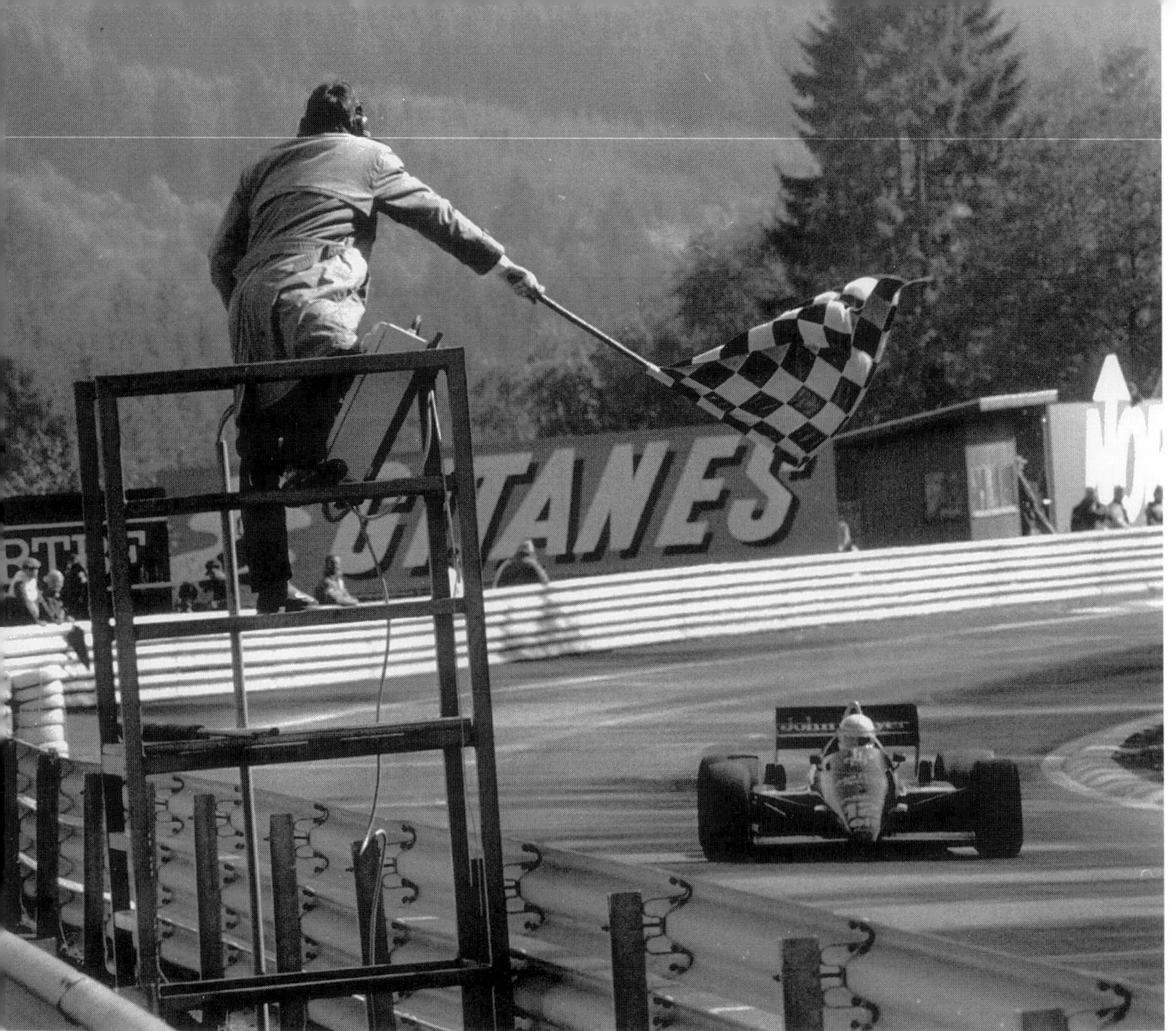

Senna takes the checkered flag to win the 1985 Belgian Formula One Grand Prix. He and his JPS Renault led from the start of the race to the finish.

Senna captured the Sao Paulo Junior championship. He won various championship titles in 1975 and 1976 before becoming the Pan American champion in 1977. Then, in 1979 and 1980, he finished second in the World Karting Championships.

After his great success in the karting world, Senna moved on to full-size race cars. In 1981, he made his debut in the Formula Ford series with the Van Deimen team. At first he wasn't too keen on racing the cars, which looked like smaller, open-wheeled versions of Formula One styleracers. Anyone watching, however, would never have known he had any hesitation whatsoever. He won 12 of the 20 races he entered that season and earned the series' Townsend-Thoresen Championship.

A year later, Senna moved up to the Formula Ford 2000 division, which used larger engines than he had run the previous season. Senna totally dominated the division, earning 16 wins in the 19 races on the British circuit and six more on the European circuit to win both the British and European championships. His popularity in the Formula Ford circuits earned him a trial Formula Three race at the end of the 1982 season, which he also won.

His great showing in the Formula Three race earned him respect and admiration from team owners who promptly moved to sign him to a long-term contract. One of those offers came from Ron Dennis of the McLaren Formula One team. Dennis wanted Senna to drive his Formula Three car, with the understanding that the deal would lead to a full-time Formula One position.

Senna, although the son of wealthy parents, realized he would need more money to compete on the Formula Three circuit. However, he also understood that if he did well—and if his past performance was any indication, he would—that Formula One teams would come knocking and he'd, in essence, have his pick of teams.

Instead, using some of his own money, Senna signed on with Dick Bennett's West Surry Formula Three team.

It was around this time that Ayrton chose to use his mother's maiden name—Senna—as his last name and dropped the full family name of da Silva.

Senna was known for his willingness to help his crew fine-tune his car.

In his first full-fledged Formula Three event at Silverstone in England, Senna recorded the second-fastest time in practice and then went on to win the event. By the end of the year, he had destroyed the competition, winning 12 of 20 races on the Formula Three circuit and the driver's championship.

Just as Senna had predicted, the offers to drive for Formula One teams came rolling in. He test drove cars for the Williams, Toleman, Brabham, and McLaren teams. Ultimately, he chose to sign with Toleman for the 1984 season.

He made his Formula One debut in his home country in the Brazil Grand Prix at Rio Jacrarepagua. In practice, he had the 16th fastest time overall. On race day, however, his car quit on the eighth lap.

During the following race in South Africa, Senna finished a respectable sixth, three laps behind the winner. At Monaco, Senna started in the 13th spot and worked his way up to second behind Alain Prost before the event was called because of rain.

Having been used to winning, and winning big, Senna grew frustrated with the Toleman operation. As a result, midway through the season, Senna started seeking another team for the following year. Before the season was over, he had signed a deal with Lotus to drive during the 1985, 1986, and 1987 season.

Senna did so without ever telling his bosses at Toleman he was pursuing another team. By not notifying the folks at Toleman, Senna had violated a rule set forth by the Formula One sanctioning body. He was banned for one race and replaced by Stefan Johannson.

Senna returned to finish out the season with Toleman and ended up ninth overall in the driver's points standings.

Although he was racing all over Europe, Senna always found time to go back home during the off-season. It was important. His parents and siblings were his support system, he often said.

The 1985 season started off again in Brazil, where Senna was able to record the fourth-fastest time in practice. Behind the wheel of a Lotus-Renault, Senna was forced out early because of an electrical problem.

Two weeks later, at the Portugal Grand Prix in Estoril, Senna mastered his Lotus and earned the pole position. Race day was rainy, but Senna drove like a champion for 67 laps and won his first Formula One race.

His first-year Lotus performance included seven pole positions and two wins. He earned the respect of his fellow drivers by finishing the season fourth in the standings.

Senna was one of the best drivers to have ever piloted a Lotus. During his three years there he earned six wins to become the most successful driver for the carmaker since Mario Andretti won the 1978 World Championship.

It was at Lotus, in 1987, that Senna helped the team's engineers develop the electronically controlled "active" suspension that would eventually make drivers more comfortable in the cars.

However, despite the technological advances, Senna sensed that the Lotus operation might be slipping. In September 1987, he announced he had signed a deal with Ron Dennis to drive for McLaren. Dennis had attempted to sign Senna several years earlier and now finally had his man. By joining McLaren, Senna acquired two-time World Champion Alain Prost as one of his new teammates.

On the track, Ayrton Senna was an aggressive driver who would push his car to the limit.

His tenacity led other drivers to complain that he was too aggressive, although they could not deny his talent. He was known as being intense and perfectionist. He was dedicated to the sport more than anyone could understand.

"All he really cares about is racing," Ron Dennis, the managing director of McLaren once said. "He is totally focused on the car, the track and the competition. There is nothing else in his life when he is at the race track."

Ayrton Senna (left) not only beat Nigel Mansell in the 1988 British Grand Prix, he also won the champagne battle on the winners' podium afterwards.

Dennis said Senna would drive "deeper in the corner than anybody, and he always knows where he is and where all the others are on the circuit."

Starting in 1988, Senna for the first time had the equipment that was equal to a driver of his caliber. At the first race in Brazil, Senna powered his McLaren-Honda to the pole position. The great starting position was wasted, however, as he was disqualified for changing cars after the start of the race.

He and the McLaren team didn't allow the first race mishap to discourage them. Indeed, at the following race, the San Marino Grand Prix at Imola, Senna again won the pole. But this time, he held on and won.

Senna earned the pole for the first six races; he won three and finished second in two others. Throughout the season he battled teammate

Alain Prost, dubbed "The Professor" by his competitors for his analytical approach to racing.

Senna's top-flight performance continued as the season progressed; he notched wins at the British Grand Prix, the German Grand Prix, the Hungary Grand Prix, and the Belgium Grand Prix. Going into the Japan Grand Prix, the next-to-last race of the season, Senna was in a position to clinch the title. He put his McLaren-Honda on the pole for the race and appeared a shoe-in for a win.

But as he led the field to the starting line, the engine on Senna's car stalled. Frustrated, he threw his arms in the air as Prost took the lead. "It was only the start that I missed all year and it was the most important one," Senna said afterwards. "I thought this is over, I am going to have to drive as hard as I can but it will be impossible to catch Alain."

Senna got the car started and immediately attacked the raceway. Each lap he gained on his rival. All was not well for Prost, either. He had gearbox problems and was losing ground. As the field passed by the pits, Senna passed Prost and took the lead for good.

Whenever he was asked about his most memorable moment, clinching the title during the 1988 Japan Grand Prix was always Senna's first choice.

Having locked up the championship in Japan, Senna was much less intense when the series rolled into Adelaide, Australia, for the season-ending Australian Grand Prix.

"With all the pressure and the stress, the season has been much too long," he said before the race. "Now that the search for the title is over, though, I feel much lighter now than I ever felt before."

Off the track Senna was not known as a driver who would spend much time speaking with the press. He learned English early and when speaking would take great pains to make his point clear. He knew comments could easily be twisted, so he made it virtually impossible for reporters to miss his point.

When asked about the potential for death in the sport, Senna was equally as precise. He put his faith in God, he said. "If you have God on your side," he said, "everything becomes clear. I have a blessing from him. But, of course, I can get hurt or killed as anyone can."

On the track he was superior. Observers of the sport said he had a flawless driving technique, which, combined with an incredible belief in himself, made him stand out.

He also took great physical care of himself. He had a strict health program devised by his personal trainer, who also coached the Brazilian volleyball team.

Senna once admitted that his devotion and focus in the car occasionally took him to a different place mentally, which couldn't be easily explained. In an interview with a Canadian writer, Senna recalled his qualifying run for the 1988 Monaco Grand Prix in vivid terms most drivers would understand.

"Suddenly, I realized that I was no longer driving consciously," he said. "I was driving it by kind of instinct, only I was on a different dimension. It was like I was in a tunnel. . . . I was just going and going, more and more and more. I was way over the limit but still able to find even more. Then suddenly something just kicked me. I kind of woke up and realized that I was in a different atmosphere than you normally are. My immediate reaction was to back off, slow down. I drove back slowly to the pits and I didn't want to go out anymore that day. It frightened me because I was well beyond my conscious understanding. It happens rarely but I keep those experiences very much alive inside me because it is something that is important for self-preservation."

Unlike some drivers who totally ignore the mechanics and engineers who built their cars, Senna was always talking with the engineers. Indeed, on race weekends, he often spent hours talking into the night with team workers.

A year after his World Championship performance, Senna found himself in a tight battle with Prost for the 1989 title. Prost eventually earned the crown, although they tangled several times on the track.

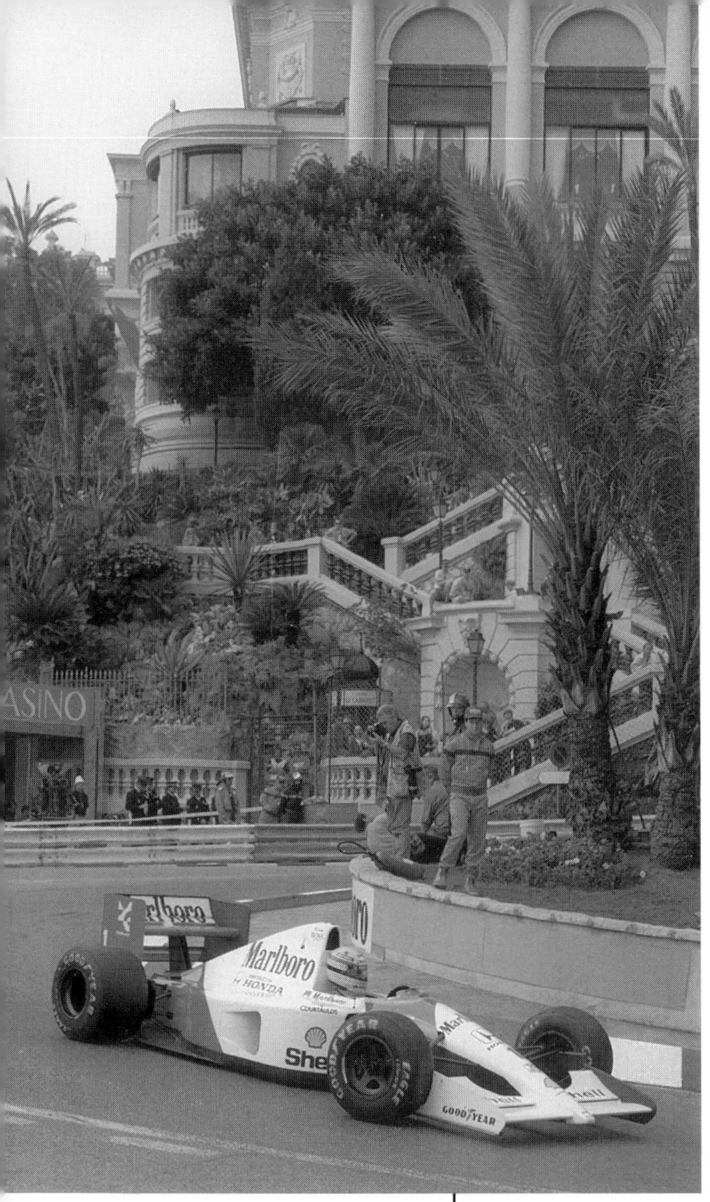

In 1991, Senna steered his McLaren-Honda to his 56th pole position at the Monaco Grand Prix.

While competitors respected Senna, they also despised him for several on-track incidents many said were examples of unsportsmanlike conduct. Indeed, during the 1990 Japan Grand Prix, with Prost in dire need of points for the driver's title, Senna rammed the back of his car and took both drivers out of the race. Senna went on to claim his second World Championship title.

As Senna's prowess on the track grew, so did his business savvy away from racing. In 1990, he stopped signing multi-year contracts, choosing to go with one-year deals that would allow him to shop his services around to the highest bidder.

Senna had many corporate ventures and ran them from an office tower in Sao Paulo, which was equipped with a helicopter landing pad on its roof. He eventually owned both Audi and Ford dealerships, had a mountain bike named after him, owned a comic book that was based on his racing exploits, and owned a household appliance plant. He also owned houses in Sao Paulo, Portugal, and Monte Carlo.

Senna was able to repeat as World Champion in 1991, a feat only a few others in the history of Formula One could match. He dropped to fourth overall in 1992 as Nigel Mansell dominated.

In 1993, McLaren and Honda parted ways. Senna sensed that loss of the power plant that had helped make him a world champion would have a major impact on the team. Ever the businessman, Senna made an unusual contractual arrangement with Ron Dennis. Instead of a year-long contract, Senna agreed to driving for a set figure of $1 million each race weekend.

Behind the wheel of a McLaren-Ford, Senna won four races and finished the 1993 season in second place behind his archrival Prost, who was now driving for the Williams-Renault team.

At the end of the 1993 season, Prost retired. Senna, without a contract at McLaren, took the opportunity to move to the Williams-Renault team. With Prost gone, Senna would stand alone. Also, the Williams-Renault operation was the very best in the business. The best car would now be paired with the best driver in all of Formula One racing.

Senna started the 1994 season with a pole position at the Brazil Grand Prix in Sao Paulo. However, his car gave out on lap 55. At the next race, the Pacific Grand Prix, Senna was on the pole. This time Senna tangled with Mika Hakkinen on the very first lap of the race and was forced out.

Ayrton Senna entered the 1994 Formula One season at the top of his craft.

Armed with three World Championship titles, he was indisputably the best driver racing on the most competitive racing series in the world. The 34-year-old handsome bachelor from Brazil was an intense driver able to squeeze more out of a car than anyone else.

His archrival and on-track nemesis, Alain Prost, the 1993 champion, had retired before the season started. Prost had collected 51 wins during his tenure and many times engaged in fierce battles with Senna on the race track. Also gone was Nigel Mansell, the 1992 World Champion who had left Formula One to race on the Indy Car circuit.

With Prost and Mansell out of the picture, Formula One belonged to Senna. He was the only World Champion still active on the series. His closest competitor was Michael Schumacher, ten years Senna's junior, who was a viable challenger for the title, although he didn't possess the seasoning of the Brazilian.

Many racing prognosticators had already

awarded Senna the championship before the first race. He was the all-around best driver in the best cars on the circuit, they argued. No one would come close.

Senna looks tired as he adjusts the rearview mirror of his McLaren Ford before the 1993 French Grand Prix.

Despite his revered position in the sport, Senna wasn't happy. A dedicated professional, Senna had grown concerned about recent changes by the sport's governing body. Changes, he felt, that had dramatically increased the risk for disaster.

Prior to the start of the season, the International Auto Racing Federation moved to take away the electronic aids that had become a part of Formula One cars. At issue was an electronic suspension system that replaced traditional springs. Without the electronic system, the cars would be very fast and difficult to drive, he said.

"It's going to be a season with lots of accidents and I'll risk saying we'll be lucky if something really serious doesn't happen," he told a Brazilian newspaper early in the season.

Senna's prediction for disaster became a reality in late April and early May 1994 when the Formula One circuit descended upon Imola, Italy, for the San Marino Grand Prix at the Ferrari Autodrome.

During practice for the race on April 30, Brazilian Rubens Barrichello lost control of his car, crashed into a tire barrier, and flew into a chain-link fence. He suffered a slight concussion.

However, the trouble did not stop there. A day later while qualifying for the race, 31-year-old Roland Ratzenberger, preparing for only his third Formula One event with a new team, slipped off the track and slammed into a cement barrier. He died.

Ratzenberger's death shocked the drivers. Followers of the sport had to look back 12 years in the record books to find another driver's race-related death. Most of them couldn't conceive of how a fellow driver could be killed. Several, including Senna, declined to continue qualifying.

In a race-day column that appeared in the German newspaper, Welt am Sonntag, Senna wrote: "My car reacts nervously to this kind of race surface. This stems from its special aerodynamics but it's also got to do with a difficulty in the suspension."

In the column, which was based on Senna's responses to a series of questions, he also said the sport needed to "look more critically at the capabilities of young or inexperienced drivers."

He said his fears were born out in tragic fashion. "I know from my own experience that as a young driver one goes into a race in a totally different way and accepts risks that you shake your head at later," Senna said.

On May 1, the San Marino Grand Prix got off as planned. At the start, J. J. Lehto of Finland stalled. As the field scrambled to get by, Lehto was rammed by Pedro Lamy of Portugal. Two wheels from Lamy's car broke off and flew into the crowd of spectators, injuring several.

The race continued under the yellow flag. Senna was the leader followed by Schumacher. When the green flag returned, Senna stormed ahead with Schumacher right behind him.

Running at about 192 mph, Senna entered a high-speed left-hand corner. His car, which should have turned, kept going straight. He slammed into an unprotected concrete wall. At the point of contact, he'd slowed the car to 131 mph, according to in-car computer data.

"He looked nervous from the very first lap," Schumacher said. "He took two or three bumps, but I can't say exactly what happened."

Senna was unconscious when rescue crews arrived. Television viewers around the world and fans trackside watched in horror as his severely injured body was put into a helicopter for a 10-minute trip to a hospital in Bologna. Hours later, doctors pronounced him dead.

When the wreckage was cleared, the drivers, unaware of Senna's condition, continued racing. Schumacher won the race, his third of the season.

An official 500-page report released nearly a year later was unable to pinpoint the exact cause of the accident. The report stated that Senna was killed by a piece of the car's suspension which punctured the cockpit.

At the time of his death, Senna had won 41

Brazilians were stunned to hear of Senna's death. The headlines here read: "Brazil Cries for Senna," "Senna Dies," and "Assassin Track Kills Senna."

races in 161 Grand Prix starts. He had 23 second place finishes, 16 third-place finishes, and seven fourths. His 41 wins stand second to Prost's record 51. His name stands atop the list of pole positions earned with 65. The second-place position on the list is held by retired driver Jim Clark who earned 33. His rival Prost only collected 33 during his career. Only two other drivers have won more World Championship titles.

Senna died as Brazil's highest-paid athlete. His salary exceeded $20 million from racing alone. Today, licensing of the Senna name for all sorts of products is a $350 million annual business.

In Brazil, Senna was a national hero. Television networks interrupted regular programming to broadcast the news. Newspapers, radio, and people on the street were talking, and weeping, over the loss.

"All Brazilians feel this death as if it were a relative," said a newsman, broadcasting word of Senna's death on television in Brazil. "Ayrton Senna, after [soccer star] Pele, is the country's biggest hero."

Senna was buried in Sao Paulo, Brazil, on May 5, 1994. An estimated one million people turned out to pay their respects to the fallen hero. Sirens wailed, confetti dropped from skyscrapers and tears flowed freely from people watching as a funeral procession carrying the body of Senna moved slowly through the streets of Sao Paulo.

"Ayrton and I shared some of the most exciting races ever staged and it's impossible to put into words what a sad loss to motor racing this is," Mansell said at the time.

Brazil's President, Itamar Franco, declared three days of national mourning and decorated Senna posthumously with the Grand Cross of Merit, one of the country's highest awards.

"He might have been the greatest driver of all time," said Michael Andretti, Senna's Formula One teammate in 1993. "There was not a weakness in Ayrton Senna."

Even now, years after his death, visitors to his grave site in Sao Paulo leave flowers, rings, beer, and champagne for their hero.

"To survive in Grand Prix racing you need to be afraid," he once said. "Fear is a very important feeling to have. It helps you stay together. It helps you race longer. . . . and live longer."

In death, Senna's name lives on as one of the greatest ever.

PLAYER'S LTD.
PPG
PLAYER'S LTD.
KLEIN TOOLS
BOSCH
Ford
sparco

JACQUES VILLENEUVE

Jacques Villeneuve was destined to become a race car driver. Some might say it was in his genes.

Born on April 9, 1971, he was the first child of Gilles and Joann Villeneuve. A sister, Melanie, was born two years later. The family lived in St.-Jean-sur-Richelieu, Quebec, which is east of Montreal.

When he was five years old, Jacques sat on his father's lap and helped steer the family car at 60 miles an hour. His father didn't need the help—he was a driver for the famed Ferrari Formula One team.

Gilles Villeneuve was born on January 18, 1950, in St.-Jean-sur-Richelieu, Quebec. Like his son, Gilles got his first taste of speed sitting on the lap of his father.

Gilles started out racing snowmobiles in Cana-

Jacques Villeneuve celebrates with his crew after winning the Indianapolis 500 in 1995. At age 24, Villeneuve was the youngest driver—as well as the first Canadian—to win the most famous Indy car race.

da. He earned the Quebec championship in 1971 and 1972 and then took the Canadian Championship in 1973. He then shifted his passion for speed to cars. In 1973, in his rookie year, Gilles won the Quebec Ford championship. He then jumped to the Formula Atlantic series, often a stepping stone to Formula One or Indy car racing. During the 1976 season he won nine out of the ten races he entered.

Gilles moved to Formula One racing in 1977 after being signed by the legendary Ferrari operation. In a world where excess is normal, Gilles' only contract demand was that his family travel with him to each of the Formula One sites.

On the track, Gilles earned a reputation for being a fearless driver with an aggressive style that occasionally got him into trouble. He won his first Formula One race in the last event of the 1977 season, which was, appropriately, the Canadian Grand Prix. He moved his family to Europe in 1978 as his career took off.

By 1982 Jacques had stopped watching his father race. "He was old enough to be aware of the danger and it made him nervous," Joann Villeneuve once told a reporter. "But, you know, if you are afraid of spiders as a child it does not mean that you will be afraid of them for the rest of your life."

Gilles Villeneuve was killed on May 8, 1982, during a qualifying session for the Belgian Grand Prix.

As a child, Jacques Villeneuve had the world at his fingertips. His mother used funds from his father's estate to move the family to Monaco, the tiny country that is home to megastars of the sports and entertainment worlds. He went to private school in Switzerland.

But Jacques couldn't shake his desire to race. When he was 15, Villeneuve attended a three-day race-driving course at the Jim Russell Racing Drivers School in Mont-Tremblant, Canada. His father had also attended the same facility. The following year, Jacques went to the Spenard-David Racing School, where he worked on his skills under Richard Spenard, a former teammate of his father's in the Atlantic Series.

Gilles Villeneuve, Jacques's father, was a racer himself. Here he holds the Challenge Trophy after winning the Formula One Race of Champions at Brands Hatch, England, in 1979.

Jacques' racing career turned serious in 1988 when he piloted an Alfa Romeo touring car in Italy. A year later, at 17, he gave up a promising professional skiing career and devoted his attention full-time to racing. He progressed to the Italian Formula Three Championship series, a tough division which serves as a proving ground for upcoming race drivers.

He spent three years in the Italian series, placing sixth overall in his final season. In 1992, he moved to Japan, where he competed in the Japanese Formula Three division. He won three races that year and finished second in the championship for Team Tom's Toyota.

"Jacques always wanted to be a race car driver," his mother once said. "Part of it comes from having grown up with it. I never discouraged him, but I did try to give him as many different options as I could."

Unlike his father, who was known for his outspoken, often cocky style, Jacques is more sedate, even cool. Some racing insiders say he's shy, while others speculate that Jacques shuns the spotlight because he doesn't want to face the questions about his father that ultimately come up in every interview.

"I could never surpass what he has done," he told a reporter who had asked about his dad. "I could win 20 championships and he would still be out there in the stars."

On another occasion, he simply replied: "I don't race for my dad," he said. "I'm happy to be his son, proud to be so. But I don't race for that. I do it for myself."

Villeneuve's big break occurred in 1993 when he was hired by Barry Green, then part owner of Forsythe-Green Ralt Racing Team which fielded cars in the Toyota Atlantic Championship series. As he had in each division before, Villeneuve outperformed everyone. In 15 races, he earned seven pole positions and won five races. He was named the series Rookie of the Year.

Forsythe-Green and Villeneuve moved up to the big leagues in 1994 when they launched a full-scale Indy car effort. Jacques' car would carry the number 27, the same number as his father's car.

Villeneuve started 15 of the 16 events on the 1994 Indy car schedule. As a rookie, he finished second in the Indianapolis 500, the best-known race in all of motorsports. He scored his first win in the 14th race of the season on the twisting road course at Road America in Elkhart Lake, Wisconsin.

Paul Tracy started on the pole and led a majority of the race. Villeneuve and Al Unser, Jr. pressured Tracy for most of the day. Villeneuve gave up second when he stalled during a pit stop. Then, with 15 laps to go and under a caution, Villeneuve plotted his strategy.

Sitting in third when the green flag dropped, Villeneuve passed both Tracy and Unser as the cars went into the first turn. He went for the inside, while Unser went for the outside. Tracy tried to close down the inside gap and hit Villeneuve's left rear tire.

"I thought that would be the best chance for me to pass," Villeneuve said. "I was quicker than them on the straights, but I couldn't get close enough to pass because I would lose downforce when I was behind them. "

Unser, who was racing for the points championship, couldn't risk messing up and losing valuable track position. Tracy, who was mathematically out of contention for the title, had little to lose.

With six laps to go, Tracy's motor expired. Unser then took off after Villeneuve. But his car wasn't fast enough. Villeneuve held on for his first Indy car win. Unser's teammate, Emerson Fittipaldi, a former two-time Formula One champion, finished third.

"He did a fantastic job," Fittipaldi said of the 23-year-old Villeneuve. "The last 10 laps with pressure from Al and me, he never made a mistake. He showed a lot of maturity, just like at Indianapolis. Jacques is more consistent than Gilles. Gilles seemed to be more up and down while Jacques is very consistent."

Actually, Villeneuve had almost made a serious error. His car ran out of fuel as he crossed the finish line.

That didn't matter. Along with the win, Villeneuve earned the series' Rookie of the Year title. In doing so, he became one of only four drivers to win a race and the Rookie title in the same season since the Indy Car World Series was formed in 1979. He finished sixth in the 1994 points battle; however, his end of season momentum meant something more. The sports world was starting to take notice of a young Canadian's rising auto racing career.

With the 1994 season barely over, Jacques Villeneuve was a wanted man. Other Indy car teams sought to sign him to a new contract as did a handful of Formula One teams.

At the finish line, it looks as if Arie Luyendyk is coming in ahead of Villeneuve at the 1995 Indianapolis 500. But Villeneuve was the winner as Luyendyk was a lap behind.

"I believe the Indy car series is a better championship with more chances to win for more drivers and teams," Villeneuve said. "But in racing, things change so fast you cannot predict the future." Barry Green knew that, too, and moved quickly to rehire Villeneuve for the 1995 campaign.

Green took over the team, renaming it Team Green, and praised his friend and on-track partner. At 23, Villeneuve was the youngest driver on the circuit. Indeed, Villeneuve, whose boyish good looks were often accented by a pair of glasses, earned the nickname: "The Baby-Faced Assassin."

"Jacques is one of the most gifted young drivers I have ever worked with," Green said. "Our growing experience, together with an extensive and aggressive testing program, should make the team a serious challenger for the title next year."

Villeneuve and Team Green didn't waste much time basking in the glow of their strong performance in the 1994 season. In fact, they held their first test in October and then tested again in December in anticipation for the season-opening race on the streets of Miami.

But testing didn't go well for Villeneuve and Green. The results were lower than anticipated, thereby cutting the team's confidence level going into Miami. Yet if he lacked confidence in his machinery, Villeneuve didn't show it when he was on the track.

Polesitter Michael Andretti dominated the first half of the Miami race, although he was sidelined early when his suspension failed. Villeneuve took the lead two-thirds of the way through the 90-lap race after a super-quick pit stop.

Under heavy pressure from Mauricio Gugelmin, Bobby Rahal, and Scott Pruett, Villeneuve didn't flinch. He held on to win the race, the second of his less than two-year-old Indy car career.

"We didn't have a good winter," he said. "We had our problems in testing. I thought we'd be strong in the race but I didn't think so much that we would have a chance to win.

"It's a great feeling," he continued. "We finished last season on a high note and we've started the season on a higher note. So we're looking forward to a great season."

Villeneuve continued to do well in the points race, scoring solid finishes in the next four races leading up to the May 28 Indianapolis 500.

Villeneuve qualified in the fifth spot—second row center—for the 79th Indianapolis 500, with an average speed of 228.397 mph. A year earlier, he had started fourth en route to his second-place finish.

"Last year, the whole month was something new," he said after qualifying for the race. "This year doesn't feel as fast as last year."

At 11 AM on May 28, the green flag dropped and the race was on. On lap 37 the yellow flag flew for the second time so track workers could clean debris from the second turn of the 2.5 mile-long oval.

However, as the field came around to take the green flag again, Villeneuve mistakenly passed the pace car and was penalized two laps. By lap 66 he made up one of those laps and by lap 120 he was back on the same lap as the rest of the field.

Villeneuve took the lead on lap 156, becoming the first driver to lead back-to-back Indy 500s since Teo Fabi did it in 1983 and 1984. On lap 185 the caution flag was out again and the field bunched up behind the pace car. Scott Goodyear, a fellow Canadian in a seemingly faster car, was ahead of Villeneuve. When the green flag dropped to restart the race on lap 190, Goodyear went too fast and passed the pace car before it could turn into the pits. Goodyear was black flagged—meaning he had to go into the pits—putting Villeneuve in the lead, a lead he did not relinquish for the final 10 laps of the race.

"I felt really happy even though we weren't in the lead because we came back from two laps down," Villeneuve said. "To win the race after that is a great feeling."

"We were down in the dumps," said Barry Green. "They took two laps from us and we got on the radio and said 'listen, guys, we're not out of this yet.' Jacques drove hard when we asked him to. He conserved fuel when we asked him to. He just did an amazing job."

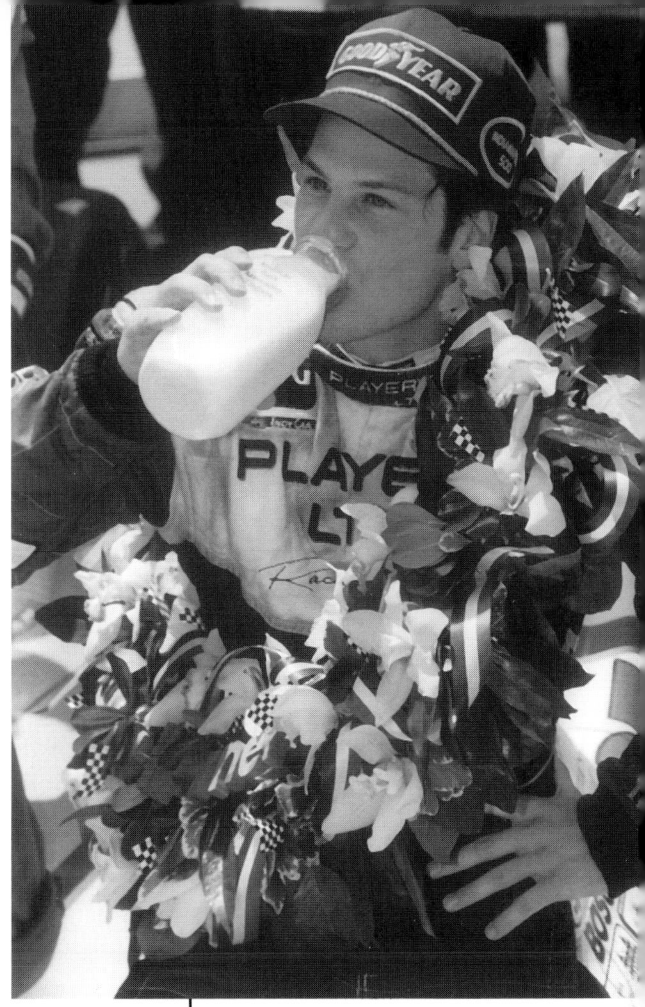

Villeneuve partakes of the traditional drink of milk after Indy, wearing the traditional winner's wreath.

Despite the $1,312,019 in prize money, there was a dark cloud hanging over Villeneuve's win. Only six races into the 17-race season, it was becoming clear to Green and those around the racing community that the young star would probably leave Indy car racing and follow his father's footsteps into Formula One.

"I'd be happy to stay with this team," Villeneuve said following Indy. "To make a big decision like that, you need to have all the cards in your hands and we just don't have all the cards."

Green hoped to talk Villeneuve out of the decision, though he seemed resigned to the fact he'd soon be looking for a replacement driver. He fended off previous suitors, although this time he wasn't feeling too positive. "I think we're going to lose him to Formula One," Green said. "He's that good."

Villeneuve went on to take the checkered flag at the Texaco Havoline 200 in July and then again at the Medic Drug Grand Prix of Cleveland two weeks later.

In early August during an off week, Villeneuve flew to England for a three-day test for the Williams-Renault Formula One team at Silverstone. Williams-Renault is one of the top teams on the Formula One circuit, and its top driver, Michael Schumacher, was moving on to anoth-

Villeneuve immediately started tearing up the courses once he got behind the wheel of Formula One racers. Here he takes his Williams-Renault out for a test drive in France.

er team. Williams-Renault wanted Villeneuve. At Silverstone he impressed the team owner by being third-fastest out of ten cars testing. He ran over 180 laps during the three-day period.

For the most part, Indy cars and Formula One vehicles are more similar than they are different. Both are single-seat vehicles equipped with engines capable of producing around 750 horsepower. Indy cars weigh more and rely heavily on ground effects—wings and spoilers—that use air under the car to create suction and keep the car on the track. Formula One cars, without such devices, provide less handling and a rougher ride for the drivers. Also, Indy cars race on both oval tracks and road courses, while the Formula One cars race exclusively on road courses spread throughout the globe.

Villeneuve said the Silverstone test was "very conclusive" and that he and the Williams-Renault team worked well together. On August

10, Villeneuve's manager Craig Pollack notified Green he would leave the Indy car series at season's end to join the Williams-Renault Formula One operation.

"It is with mixed emotions that we have learned of Jacques' decision," Green said. "Obviously, we are saddened to lose Jacques as a member of our team but at the same time we are proud that we have made a significant contribution to his development." Green said then that Villeneuve would be a star in Formula One.

While he was going Formula One racing in 1996, Villeneuve never let up on the Indy car series in 1995. "It's not that you prepare yourself," he once said when asked how he was balancing the Indy car series and his future Formula One deal. "It's just that if you do something, you do it 100%. You don't do it for half. And we are still fighting for the championship."

With that same determination, he secured the series championship by finishing 11th at the Toyota Monterey Grand Prix. In doing so he became the youngest champion in series history.

"This is my first championship in any series so it is special," Villeneuve said. "It's only North America, but it is a top class series, so to win the championship means a lot."

However, Villeneuve, the champion, had already announced he would not be returning for another season on the Indy car circuit. His decision to go to Formula One racing had already been made.

"It's never easy with a big decision," he said of the move to Formula One. "But in a way it was a golden opportunity. The timing was perfect. All of the top contenders in Formula One are signing long term deals. . . so there wouldn't be a big door open like there would this year."

Villeneuve said making the decision was hard because of the relationship he had developed with team owner Barry Green and the rest of his crew members. Indeed, it took the team a couple of weeks to accept his decision, he said.

After the 1995 season, Villeneuve moved to Monaco, where his family now lives, and set out to acclimate to the Formula One world. He said he'd have no difficulty adjusting to the Formula One culture because that was the environment in which he was raised. Learning the characteristics of the car would be accomplished by midwinter. Learning the tracks he'd never raced on would be the biggest hurdle, he said.

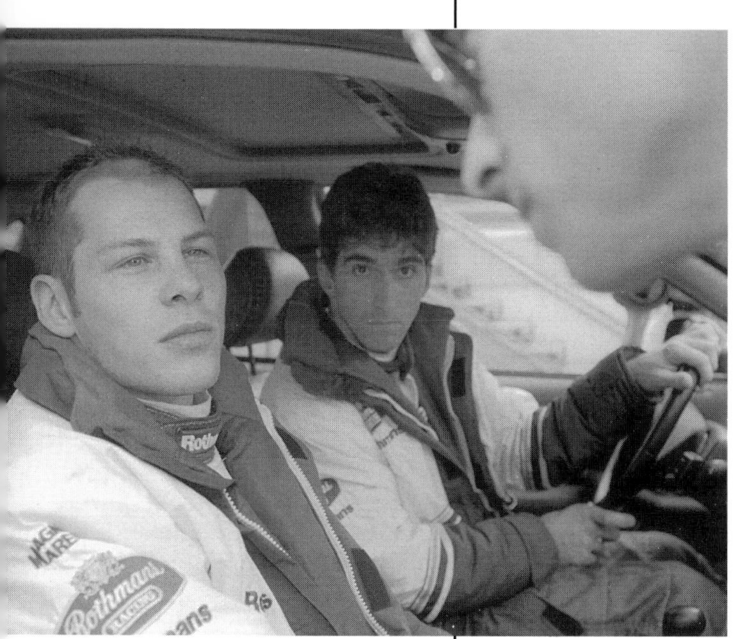

Jacques Villeneuve (left) and Damon Hill—teammates and rivals for the World Championship—checked out track conditions at Estoril, Portugal, in 1996.

"I am going there to fight," Villeneuve said, "not to be impressed by everything and say 'oh wow, that's incredible.' I am not going there either to just go around the track and see what happens. I am going out there to fight like [I have during] the Indy season this year."

And fight he did. Using a motorsports video game, Villeneuve was able to learn some tracks well enough to earn the pole position at a couple of races. When the season ended, he had won four races. In fact, entering the final event in Japan, Villeneuve had an outside chance at beating teammate Damon Hill for the driver's championship. However, a bad tire ended his day early. He finished second to Hill for the championship.

Villeneuve, in just one season, had again let the sports world take notice. He was no longer driving in the shadow of his father and was a force to be reckoned with.

When the green flag dropped, indicating the start of the European Grand Prix in Nurburgring, Germany, Jacques Villeneuve stormed into the lead. It was April 29, 1996, and a cool and sunny afternoon—perfect racing weather. The race marked Villeneuve's fourth-ever Formula One race. He started on the front row, alongside first-place starter and teammate Damon Hill.

"Once again a new circuit, but I've not done too badly so far and I'm looking forward to the challenge," Villeneuve said of Nurburgring after finishing second to Hill in the previous race in Argentina. "I've really enjoyed those opening three races and I can see no reason why that will not continue once we start racing in Europe."

Villeneuve was not boasting. Just four races into his rookie season on what is arguably the toughest and most competitive racing series in the world, the driver was in second place in the Formula One points standings and had already notched two second-place finishes.

Despite his relatively young age, Villeneuve had the confidence and savvy of a driver with twice his experience. However, at the European Grand Prix, none of his past records mattered. What did matter was that he was racing among some of the best drivers in the world.

At the start, Hill couldn't get his Williams-Renault moving and Villeneuve, who two weeks before had turned 25, darted into the lead. It was immediately clear that the Quebec-born driver had a firm grip on the 2.822-mile long twisting road course.

Villeneuve took the lead and never let up. Hill found himself in fifth before the first lap was over. Villeneuve showed no signs of being a rookie, though he was. For the first 24 laps, Villeneuve had a comfortable lead over David Coulthard, who was driving a McLaren-Mercedes. Coulthard started sixth, on the outside of row three in the starting grid.

Coulthard gave up the second spot when he pitted on lap 24. Then Mika Hakkinen moved into second, although he was no match for the dominant Villeneuve. On lap 26, Villeneuve stopped to have his own car serviced, although he was still in the lead when he returned to the track.

But midway through the race, Villeneuve's seemingly easy run was in jeopardy. In his rearview mirror was Ferrari driver Michael Schumacher, a two-time Formula One World Champion and perhaps the most aggressive and intimidating driver in the series.

Schumacher pitted for the last time on lap 44 and turned the second spot back to Coulthard. Coulthard would only hold the position for a single lap before Schumacher was back on Villeneuve's tail.

For the next 20 laps, Villeneuve coolly fought off the best moves Schumacher could make to wrestle away the lead on the very tight circuit. Schumacher tried inside and then out with no luck. Villeneuve, like a veteran racer, blocked every Schumacher attempt.

On the 67th and last lap, his lead was down to just seven-tenths of a second, but Villeneuve held on, making good on a promise he had announced in his first race of the season: to win.

"It's a great feeling to win here and get my first victory in Formula One," he said following the victory. "We finally got onto the highest step of the podium after being competitive since the beginning of the season."

Team owner Frank Williams simply said Villeneuve was "terrific."

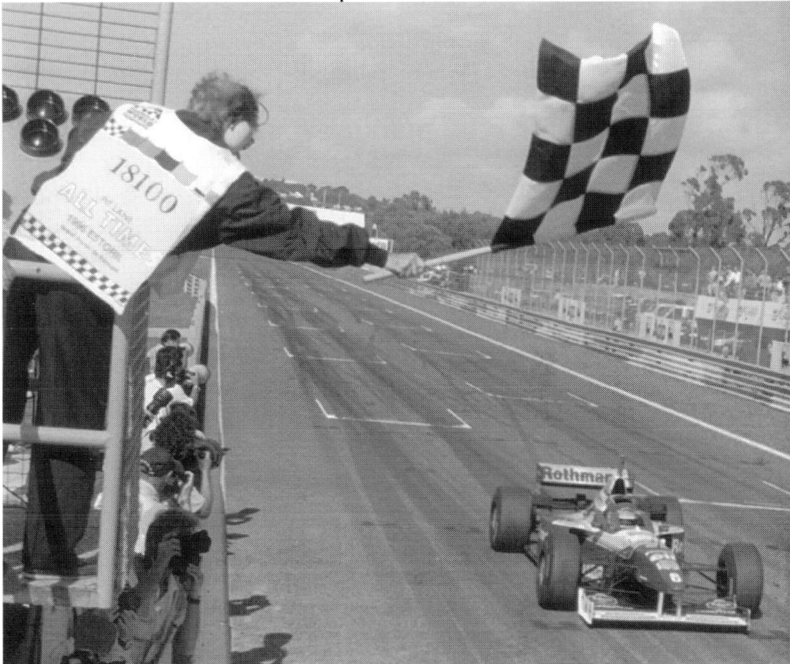

Villeneuve easily won the 1996 Portuguese Grand Prix at Estoril.

"The car was much better than in qualifying and it was particularly good after my second pit stop, which was a good thing because Michael [Schumacher] was going really strongly," Villeneuve said. "As long as there was not too much traffic I could keep an eye on Michael and see where he was. At times he was too close to be comfortable but he made it fun."

Said Schumacher, who admitted he wanted to win in his homeland: "Jacques drove a very good race and did not make the slightest mistake."

Only seven other drivers have earned their first Formula One victories earlier in their careers. Villeneuve now stands among the elite drivers. "Every win is special, especially the first in a new series like this," Villeneuve said. "But there's a long way to go in the championship and this is only one win."

CHRONOLOGY

MICHAEL SCHUMACHER

1969 born on January 3 in Hurth-Hermulheim, Germany
1985 repeats as German Junior go-karting champion
1988 drives on the FF1600 circuit, finishing second in the European division
1990 wins German Formula Three championship; wins first race outside of Europe, in Mexico, while driving for Mercedes
1991 moves up to Formula One circuit; finishes 12th in the overall standings
1994 wins six of the first seven races of the year and four more later in the season, even though he had to sit out two races for having ignored a black flag; at age 25, he is the youngest Formula One champion ever
1995 signs a $50 million deal to drive for Ferrari; wins his second championship while tying the record for most wins in a season (nine)

AYRTON SENNA

1960 born March 21, in Sao Paulo, Brazil
1974 wins Sao Paulo Junior go-karting championship
1981 wins Townsend-Thoresen Championship in Formula Ford series
1982 in an amazingly dominating fashion, wins 16 of 19 races in the British Formula Ford division; also wins European championship; enters and wins first Formula Three race
1984 debuts as a Formula One racer; finishes ninth in the overall standings
1988 wins eight races and the driver's championship
1991 performs rare feat in repeating as champion in back-to-back seasons
1993 signs to drive with Ron Dennis for $1 million per race weekend; finishes second in the overall standings
1994 wins his 41st race, putting him second on all-time list; on May 1, dies in a crash during the running of the San Marino Grand Prix

JACQUES VILLENEUVE

1971 born on April 9, in St.-Jean-sur-Richelieu, Canada
1982 Gilles Villeneuve, Jacques's father, dies in a crash during a qualifying session for the Belgian Grand Prix
1989 drives on the Italian Formula Three circuit
1993 wins seven pole positions and five races, earning Rookie of the Year honors in the Toyota Atlantic championship series
1994 switches to Indy cars, finishing second at the Indianapolis 500 and earning Rookie of the Year honors
1995 wins Indianapolis 500 and becomes first driver in over 10 years to lead Indy two years in a row
1996 switches to Formula One racing and wins the driver's championship, becoming the youngest champion in series history

SUGGESTIONS FOR FURTHER READING

Henry, Alan, *Grand Prix Champions from Jackie Stewart to Michael Schumacher.* Osceola, WI: Motorbooks International, 1995

Hilton, Christopher, *Jacques Villeneuve, In His Own Right.* London: Patrick Stevens, Ltd., 1996

Hilton, Christopher, *Ayrton Senna, His Full Racing Record.* London: Patrick Stevens, Ltd., 1995

Hilton, Christopher, *Michael Schumacher, Defending the Crown.* London: Patrick Stevens Ltd., 1995

ABOUT THE AUTHOR

Richard Huff is an award-winning journalist and author of *Behind The Wall: A Season on the NASCAR Circuit.* He is a staff writer and motor sports columnist for the *New York Daily News.* He is also a contributing writer and columnist for *NASCAR Truck Racing Magazine.* He lives in Highlands, N.J., with his wife and son.

INDEX

PHOTO CREDITS
AP/Wide World Photos: 2, 8, 11, 15, 17, 22, 25, 28, 30, 35, 38, 41, 55, 56, 59, 61; Bettmann: 46, 49, 52; Archive Photos: 18, 32, 44